6/06

22.95

D0570743

CROSSING THE SEAS
Americans Form an Empire (1890-1899)

TITLE LIST

CROSSING THE SEAS
Americans Form an Empire (1890-1899)

BY
ERIC SCHWARTZ

MASON CREST PUBLISHERS
PHILADELPHIA

Mason Crest Publishers Inc.
370 Reed Road
Broomall, Pennsylvania 19008
(866) MCP-BOOK (toll free)

Copyright © 2005 by Mason Crest Publishers. All rights reserved. No part
of this publication may be reproduced or transmitted in any form or by
any means, electronic or mechanical, including photocopying, recording,
taping, or any information storage and retrieval system, without
permission from the publisher.

First printing
1 2 3 4 5 6 7 8 9 10

Library of Congress Cataloging-in-Publication Data

Schwartz, Eric.
  Crossing the seas : Americans form an empire (1890–1899) / by Eric Schwartz.
    p. cm. — (How America became America)
  ISBN 1-59084-910-8 1-59084-900-0 (series)
 1. United States—Foreign relations—1865–1898—Juvenile literature. 2. United States—Territorial
expansion—Juvenile literature. 3. Imperialism—History—19th century—Juvenile literature. I.
Title. II. Series.
  E661.7.S39 2005
  325'.32'097309034—dc22
                                    2004027341

Design by Dianne Hodack and MK Bassett-Harvey.
Produced by Harding House Publishing Service, Inc.
Cover design by Dianne Hodack.
Printed in the Hashemite Kingdom of Jordan.

973,8
SCH
2005

CONTENTS

INTRODUCTION

by Dr. Jack Rakove

Today's America is not the same geographical shape as the first American colonies—and the concept of America has evolved as well over the years.

When the thirteen original states declared their independence from Great Britain, most Americans still lived within one or two hours modern driving time from the Atlantic coast. In other words, the Continental Congress that approved the Declaration of Independence on July 4, 1776, was continental in name only. Yet American leaders like George Washington, Benjamin Franklin, and Thomas Jefferson also believed that the new nation did have a continental destiny. They expected it to stretch at least as far west as the Mississippi River, and they imagined that it could extend even further. The framers of the Federal Constitution of 1787 provided that western territories would join the Union on equal terms with the original states. In 1803, President Jefferson brought that continental vision closer to reality by purchasing the vast Louisiana Territory from France. In the 1840s, negotiations with Britain and a war with Mexico brought the United States to the Pacific Ocean.

This expansion created great opportunities, but it also brought serious costs. As Americans surged westward, they created a new economy of family farms and large plantations. But between the Ohio River and the Gulf of Mexico, expansion also brought the continued growth of plantation slavery for millions of African Americans. Political struggle over the extension of slavery west of the Mississippi was one of the major causes of the Civil War that killed hundreds of thousands of Americans in the 1860s but ended with the destruction of slavery. Creating opportunities for American farmers also meant displacing Native Americans from the lands their ancestors had occupied for centuries. The opening of the west encouraged massive immigration not only from Europe but also from Asia, as Chinese workers came to labor in the California Gold Rush and the building of the railroads.

By the end of the nineteenth century, Americans knew that their great age of territorial expansion was over. But immigration and the growth of modern industrial cities continued to change the American landscape. Now Americans moved back and forth across the continent in search of economic opportunities. African Americans left the South in massive numbers and settled in dense concentrations in the cities of the North. The United States remained a magnet for immigration, but new immigrants came increasingly from Mexico, Central America, and Asia.

Ever since the seventeenth century, expansion and migration across this vast landscape have shaped American history. These books are designed to explain how this process has worked. They tell the story of how modern America became the nation it is today.

The British flag

One
AMERICA TAKES ON THE BRITISH EMPIRE

At some point, all children rebel against their parents. The young American nation was no exception.

America's earliest rebellion took place during the American Revolution, of course, when the thirteen colonies won their independence from England, but that was just the beginning. Once the United States took shape, the relationship between England and her upstart child continued to be strained. Over the years, Americans remained close to their roots culturally, but as in most families, tensions and conflicts often arose.

By the end of the nineteenth century, both the mother country and her offspring had grown in power. America was no longer an infant taking its first brave steps toward nationhood—and England had swelled into an empire. "The sun never sets on the English Empire," was a common saying in those days. In other words, England's colonies were scattered around the globe, so that at any hour, somewhere, the sun was shining on British land.

The American flag

The process of becoming an adult often involves imitating the parent, even as the child challenges the parent's authority. This was the case for the United States. In the final years of the nineteenth century, America began to push at the envelope of British authority—and at the same time, Americans began entertaining thoughts of building their own empire, one that would outlast and outshine England's. But to do this, they would need to challenge the longtime empires that had already *colonized* much of the globe.

The jungle of Venezuela seems like an unlikely place for the United States to face down the British Empire. But then much about the conflict that took place there in 1895 seems unlikely. Nevertheless, the incident shook

America's relationship with Great Britain—and it helped Americans expand their sense of their nation's place in the world.

The problem arose out of a minor border incident between Great Britain and Venezuela. At the end of the Napoleonic Wars, England had acquired a portion of Guiana on the northern coast of South America. From the very beginning, British Guiana's border with Venezuela to the west had been disputed. The Venezuelans claimed several hundred miles of land inside of

*A territory that has been **colonized** has been taken over and settled by another country.*

Empires

An empire exists when a government has control over lands that are separate from it, lands that once existed as independent states. One of the earliest and most powerful empires, the Roman Empire, once spread across most of Europe. Centuries later, the great European powers—Spain, England, and France—built their own empires as they colonized the "new land" they discovered in the Western Hemisphere.

When an empire absorbs a smaller and weaker country, it often brings some very real benefits to that country. Inevitably, however, the gains are balanced by losses that are just as real. According to historian Paul Schroeder, "Those who speak of an . . . empire bringing freedom and democracy to the world are talking of dry rain and snowy blackness. In principle and by definition, empire is the negation of political freedom, liberation, and self-determination."

*In **arbitration**, a third party settles disputes between two or more people or groups.*

*When countries have representatives (diplomats) in another country, they are said to have **diplomatic relations** with each other.*

British Guiana—but they offered to have the matter settled by international **arbitration**. The British, however, refused this suggestion, and the matter remained unresolved for decades. By the time President Grover Cleveland was elected as America's president for a second time in 1892, Great Britain and Venezuela had broken off **diplomatic relations**.

Cleveland worried that the British might be extending their claims in South America to include the mouth of the Orinoco River, one of the main waterways in the area. Such a claim would increase the British Empire's power and influence in the Western Hemisphere. Americans were unwilling to see that happen. They saw such a threat as a direct infringement of the Monroe Doctrine.

This principle, issued by President James Monroe in 1823, played a vital role in the way Americans viewed themselves (and it still is a major influence). Originally, the doctrine's intention was to

Map of the British Empire

The Napoleonic Wars

The years between 1804 and 1815 were ones of great conflict in Europe as a man of small stature tried to achieve large goals. Napoleon Bonaparte I of France set about to conquer Britain and all of Europe. In 1805, Bonaparte tried to invade Britain from Boulogne. Admiral Lord Horatio Nelson stopped his forces at the Battle of Trafalgar.

A year later, Napoleon attempted a blockade to isolate Britain from Europe, but that failed as well when Russia refused to cooperate. So, Napoleon decided to invade Russia, and the battle cost his troops massive casualties.

One thing that Napoleon did accomplish was the bringing together of Britain, Prussia, Russia, Austria, and Sweden. This alliance defeated the "Little Corporal" at the Battle of Nations in Leipzig, Germany. Napoleon abdicated and went to Elba.

Napoleon wasn't finished, however. He returned to Paris in 1815 and restarted his campaign. It was short-lived, and Napoleon and his troops were defeated by Arthur Wellesley, the Duke of Wellington, at the Battle of Waterloo on June 18, 1815.

limit European expansion into the Western Hemisphere. Monroe proclaimed, "the American continents, by the free and independent condition which they have assumed and maintain, are henceforth not to be considered as subjects for future colonization by any European powers." But the Monroe Doctrine went one step further: it assigned the United States the responsibility of protecting all Western nations from outside intervention. It

volved "whenever new alleged instances of British aggression upon Venezuelan territory" occurred. The actual security of the United States might be threatened, the letter implied, if "European powers may convert American states into colonies or provinces of their own."

The letter offended the British, who responded that the Monroe Doctrine had no legal standing in international law. In any case, England insisted, Venezuela's land claims lacked foundation, and so there was no reason to put the matter before an international court.

At this point, tensions grew still greater. President Cleveland was so annoyed that he asked Congress to fund a commission to investigate the matter. He claimed that Britain's actions in South America might lead to America's "loss of national self-respect and honor."

Cleveland may have had several reasons for his attitude. He may have perceived that the United States had an economic interest in ensuring that Venezuela remained in control of a river that served as transportation for American merchants. He may have also sought to solidify the United States' political power over the region. Cleveland may even have wanted to stoke the fires of **nationalism** with some harmless chest-thumping, distracting voters from the

Symbolic representation of England's growing empire

gave America the right to interfere in conflicts between other nations.

The doctrine was the justification for American involvement in Britain's conflict with Venezuela. President Cleveland's government wrote an assertive letter to Great Britain, stating that the United States was bound to become in-

Western and Eastern Hemispheres

economic problems of the time. Probably, however, his call for a commission was simply part of his overall approach to foreign affairs. Cleveland tended to be sensitive toward slights—personal or diplomatic, real or imagined—and he reacted to them emotionally. His hero was President Andrew Jackson, and like Jackson, Cleveland promoted an aggressive patriotism, even in situations that he only dimly understood. Both presidents often failed to perceive the rights of others (whether they be American Indians or African Americans, as in Jackson's case—or citizens of other nations, as was Cleveland's case).

Nationalism *is a feeling of proud loyalty and devotion to a nation.*

15

Congress quickly approved funds for the commission to study the Venezuelan border issue, but Americans' reactions were mixed. Some *financiers* were concerned about the possibility of war and how that might affect the national debt. Cleveland himself had his own doubts; he really didn't want war, but he didn't feel like he could back away from the issue.

Fortunately, the British were not eager to fight the Americans either. For the next few months, the two countries exchanged diplomatic proposals to solve the problem. Eventually, the British agreed to submit the matter to arbitration, with some limitations. The arbitration tribunal would only consider those areas of the country that had been settled by the British for less than fifty years. The concern of the British was that their subjects shouldn't suddenly find themselves Venezuelans rather than British.

The importance of the Venezuelan border incident, however, was not the tribunal's decision one way or the other. For America, at least, the incident's real value lay in the way it dramatically extended the Monroe Doctrine. In the Venezuelan border dispute, the United States for the first time claimed authority to interfere in a matter in which it was not even directly in-

James Monroe

volved. This principle would be invoked repeatedly in future interventions.

Most historians today believe that President Monroe issued his famous doctrine as a political strategy to bolster public opinion in his favor. He probably never dreamed his proclamation would take on near-biblical substance in the minds of future Americans. The philosophy behind the Monroe Doctrine shaped America's emerging sense of itself as a power great enough to stand up against its parent nation: England, the nineteenth-century world's "super power." This same philosophy would justify the United States' actions as it began to build its own empire.

> The arbitration tribunal finally handed down its decision in October 1899, more than two years after President Cleveland left office. The panel ruled that Venezuela did have ownership of the mouth of the Orinoco River, but most of the previous boundary with the British colony was deemed valid.

Financiers are people skilled in financial matters, and who usually have a great deal of personal wealth.

History is like a multifaceted jewel, made up of many perspectives. The builders of empires have exciting stories to tell, stories that are full of courage and adventure. The settlers who venture into new lands often pride themselves on their free and daring spirits, their willingness to endure hardships, their determination in the face of obstacles. From their perspective, these stories are true. But the people who already live in those same new lands know a different side to the truth. The natives' stories tell of loss and destruction, tragedy and death.

The Monroe Doctrine has played a major role in the stories the United States has told about itself—but it is only one angle of history's many facets. As America matured as a nation, the Monroe Doctrine touched the lives of countless citizens of other lands. It would lead the United States into a war; by the end of that war, America would have acquired several of the islands that sprinkled the world's oceans—including a peaceful island nation called Hawaii. Each of these places had its own story to tell.

President Grover Cleveland

17

According to mythology, the Hawaiian Islands are the children of the earth and sky.

Two
THE ANCIENT LAND OF HAWAII

In the beginning, according to the ancient Hawaiians, everything came from lipo, the black depths of the ocean. Then Papa, the earth-mother, and Wakea, the sky-father, gave birth to the islands Hawaii and Maui and to a girl whose name means "to generate stars in the sky." From subsequent unions were born the *taro* plant, staple of the Hawaiians, as well as the rest of the Hawaiian Islands.

This creation story implies fundamental elements of Hawaiian philosophy. Everything and everybody are linked together. Nothing remains the same; everything is always changing, growing, developing. The world is not inanimate and dead, but alive and breathing, full of meaning. At the same time, everything has a place. Ultimately, everything in the world is the way it should be.

SiMMS LIBRARY ALBUQUERQUE ACADEMY

Taro is a plant known for its starchy, edible tubers.

> "Everything is alive—the reflections, the shadows, the sounds, the wind, the splash of the waves on the beach. . . . And everything is communicating with us. All we need to do is open up. . . ."
> —Kekuni Blaisdell, advocate for Hawaiian independence

ing methods allowed them to feed a large population with a minimum of effort. Although the ancient Hawaiians worked only about four hours a day, they built the largest temples and the fastest canoes in all the Pacific. Their dances and poetry were sophisticated art forms, expressing deep meaning with great *eloquence*. The Hawaiians dressed in fine fabrics woven from bark, and they had never experienced diseases. They'd never even had a cold.

These insights had been handed down orally from generation to generation, in a line that stretched back to the people's most long-ago ancestors. These were members of *Polynesia*'s sophisticated societies, settlers who had come to the Hawaiian Islands as early as 100 B.C.

The ancient Hawaiians explored the entire Pacific, navigating totally by their deep understanding of the natural world, centuries before Europeans ventured out into the Atlantic. At home, the Hawaiians were expert farmers, developing more than two hundred varieties of sweet potato and taro in fields watered by complicated irrigation systems. Their efficient farm-

Native Hawaiians believe that each blossom, each ray of light, is alive and meaningful.

Like all human civilizations, the Hawaiians had their share of conflict and cruelty, but for the most part, theirs was a peaceful and productive society, ruled by tradition and deep spiritual beliefs. Nothing was done without acknowledging the presence of the gods and goddesses. Because their entire life was spiritual, they did not even have a word for "religion." According to Mary Kawena Pukui, Hawaii's most famous historian, "Everything they did, they did with prayer." *Mana* (spiritual force) was present everywhere.

Kapu (a system of sacred rules) governed the lives of these long-ago Hawaiians. According to these rules, certain actions were **taboo**; for example, men's and women's roles were carefully defined, which meant that men could only do certain kinds of work, while women did others. Men and women were not permitted to even eat and drink together. Breaking a kapu meant death.

But the ancient Hawaiians also had a system whereby a person could have a second chance. If lawbreakers (or anyone else in need of sanctuary) could reach a *pu'uhonua* (a place of refuge), they were safe, as no blood could be shed in these sacred areas. Within the refuge, people were **absolved** of all their offenses. They could then return home, innocent once more, and resume their lives.

The ancient Hawaiians' insight and wisdom was also evident in their system of land management. Unlike European cultures, the Hawaiians had no concept of land ownership. Since all things were connected, no one could own land. Instead, the land was divided into sections (*ahupua'a*), which extended from the summits of the mountains, down through the fertile valleys, to the edge of the sea. The *alii* (chiefs) were stewards of the land and granted the people living in each ahupua'a use of the land's bounty for their livelihood.

Polynesia is made up of a group of islands, including Hawaii, Samoa, and the Cook Islands, of the central and southern Pacific Ocean.

To have **eloquence** is to have the ability to communicate with forceful, expressive, and persuasive language.

Something that is **taboo** is forbidden.

Absolved means to be forgiven.

The Pacific Ocean where the Hawaiian Islands lie.

21

Ecological zones *are areas that share a common set of physical and geographical characteristics.*

Konohiki (headmen) facilitated day-to-day operations with the help of *luna* (land specialists). Each land section formed a self-contained economic and social unit that effectively integrated human beings and resources from very different ***ecological zones***. Everyone living throughout the ahupuaʻa had access to all types of products, and everyone was entitled to a share of what they produced from the soil or took from the sea. The system benefited the land because the ahupuaʻa was managed carefully, thought of and cared for as a whole. Living in harmony with the land developed into an exquisite art form for the Hawaiians; and generosity in all things, especially in the sharing of food, was considered the highest mark of civilized behavior.

The Hawaiians' peaceful and productive existence was shaken to its very roots, however, in 1778, when the British explorer Captain James Cook landed on the island of Kuai'i. Captain Cook's arrival opened the islands to the rest of the world and signaled the end of the Hawaiians' ancient culture.

A German sailor with the expedition described the first encounter between the two different cultures:

Many natives approached us in their boats. They were the most beautiful people whom we had ever seen among all the savage nations; we sought to lure them to the ship through friendly gestures and the showing of various gifts. At first they refused, and from their great astonishment manifested on account of the ships we could deduce that these people had never before seen any ships.

23

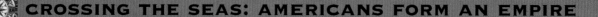

The ancient Hawaiians lived in dwellings like these.

Land sections reached from the mountains, down through the fertile valleys, to the sea coast.

24

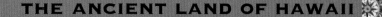

Hawaiians have never understood American and European perspectives on money and ownership. Modern activist Kekuni Blaisdell considers Western culture to be "individualistic, materialistic, and exploitive." In *Voices of Wisdom: Hawaiian Elders Speak*, he goes on to say, "Our culture is the antithesis. Instead of taking, we give. In our tradition, the fisherman catches fish not only for himself, but for everyone in the ahupuaʻa. The taro farmer harvests not only for himself, but for others in the ahupuaʻa. The woodsman up mauka [mountainside] cuts firewood and shares. Therefore, the greatest virtue and personal asset is not how much money one has in the bank, but one's relationships. That's the basis for our traditional culture."

Today, modern environmentalists view the ahupuaʻa system as an excellent model of resource management.

Traditional Hawaiian carving

About forty-five years later, Hawaiian students at a missionary school wrote this account of the same event:

> The landing took place at night at Waimea; and when it was daylight again, the people on shore saw that this strange thing had landed and they were astonished and there was great shouting.
>
> One said to the other, "What is this great branch?" Someone answered, "These are the stems of trees; they approached from the sea." And the panicking was great.
>
> Then the ali'i [chief] ordered some men to go out with a canoe and look, so that this strange object be closely examined. They went and made contact with the ship, and they saw that iron was joined to the outside of the ship, and they were happy, because there was much iron.
>
> Because iron had been known before, since timber with iron had landed before, but that had been little, and this was much. And they climbed aboard and they saw persons, their brows were white, their eyes light, their kapa [clothes] wrinkled, their heads cornered, and their speech was a gibberish.

While Cook was welcomed first as chief or god, on his last visit to the islands on February 14, 1779, he was killed by natives when he tried to take the Hawaiian ruler, King Kalani'opuu, to

Captain Cook

his ship as a hostage. This hostile action was unusual for the peaceful Hawaiians, however, and the Hawaiian *archipelago* became a favorite stop for ships en route from the northwest United States to China. Both British and American sea captains made use of the islands as a stopping place where they could stock up on provisions and fresh water.

Eighteenth-century *Westerners* were delighted with the Hawaiian Islands, just as they are today. But the encounter between the Hawaiians and outsiders did not prove to be as positive for the native population. The Europeans brought with them the forces of change and destruction. Hawaii's ancient culture could not withstand the newcomers' presence.

The Hawaiian kapu system of law was seriously challenged by the foreigners who began to arrive in Hawaii. The natives noticed that

Hawaiian boat

28

the white people who came to the islands did not abide by the rules of the kapu system—and the gods did not punish them. If the white people could break the kapu, the Hawaiians reasoned, why shouldn't they?

In 1795, the young chief, Kamehameha I (also called Kamehameha the Great) united the Hawaiian Islands (with the exception of Kauai) into a single unified kingdom. He attempted to rule his land using the ancient system of kapu—but the ongoing influx of foreigners hindered his efforts.

Encounters with Americans and Europeans also brought diseases to the Hawaiian Islands. The natives had no immunity against illnesses such as smallpox and influenza, and thousands upon thousands died as a result.

After the whalers and sailors, the missionaries soon followed, bringing Christianity to the islands. At first, the Hawaiians met them politely but coolly. After all, they had their own ancient spiritual beliefs. As their ancient belief systems unraveled, however, the people and their rulers were more receptive to a new religion. After some negotiation with the King, the missionaries obtained

*An **archipelago** is a group or chain of islands.*

***Westerners** are people, primarily in North and South America and Europe, whose culture is influenced by Greek and Roman culture and Christianity.*

In 1819, King Kamehameha II officially declared an end to the kapu system. In a dramatic and highly symbolic event, the King ate and drank with women, thereby breaking the important eating kapu. Soon after, the sacred heiau (temples) were destroyed, and the images of gods were burned. As word of these events spread throughout the Islands, the kapu system rapidly unraveled.

permission to establish a mission for a trial period of one year, provided that they teach literature and the arts in addition to the **doctrines** of their faith.

Christianity may have been the missionaries' religious faith—but they also put faith in the economic creed of **capitalism**. The Hawaiians learned the **precepts** of this faith, too. King Kamehameha II, for example, earned tidy profits from service to the sailing ships; he had accumulated 250,000 in Spanish silver dollars by the time of his death. Other rulers, however, were not so financially talented and ran up large debts. King Kamehameha III asked William Richards, an American missionary, to explain the principles of capitalism to him.

The early settlement of Honolulu by Westerners

The rules of the capitalist system, after all, went against the ancient beliefs of the Hawaiians. Capitalism by definition requires capital—accumulated goods—but the Hawaiians traditionally shared everything. For them, saving a stockpile of wealth for yourself was equivalent to *hana pi*, stinginess, which was a socially unacceptable behavior.

Although the values of Christianity and capitalism conflict with each other in many ways, William Richards knew that if the Hawaiians did not understand capitalism, the foreigners would overpower them. He was an advocate for the Hawaiian people and had sworn to defend the independence of their islands. So Richards set aside his Bible and began teaching economics.

One of his lectures concerned the concept of land as capital, and the idea that the land should be used to create wealth. Richards was the one who first suggested raising sugarcane, which had been raised for centuries in the Caribbean, as one method to

Doctrines are rules or principles that form the basis of a belief or policy.

The economic system based on free enterprise and the private ownership of the means of production is called **capitalism**.

Precepts are the rules or instructions that guide one's behavior, especially moral behavior.

Hawaiians perceive spiritual harmony in the natural world around them.

The population of the Hawaiian Islands before contact with the Europeans is estimated to be 300,000; by 1900, only 40,000 native Hawaiians remained.

Statue of Kamehameha the Great

increase the production of capital from the land. Hawaiians, Richards explained, had a natural advantage in growing a crop like sugarcane.

The first sugar mill on the islands was built in 1802, and King Kamehameha I owned a mill by 1811. These first steps into capitalism would probably have remained small, however, without changes in Hawaii's land ownership laws. The "reforms" were intended to secure the future of the native Hawaiians. Ultimately, they impoverished them instead.

Richards and his fellow missionaries were once more behind the new wave of change that swept over the Hawaiian Islands. Great Britain was threatening to lay claim to the islands, but the missionaries didn't like the idea of living under a British flag. If the King could start a program of land ownership, they reasoned, then foreign control of the islands might be avoided. The missionaries also thought that it might make the natives give up their ancient ways and conform better to the Protestant concept of a Christian lifestyle.

Eventually, the missionaries persuaded the King that if his people were given the opportunity to own their own taro patches and houses, the population would stop dropping. And if the land were equally distributed to all, then the

32

Hawaii contains many different ecosystems.

people would not be alienated from the land. The land distribution program, approved August 6, 1850, allowed the male head of every Hawaiian family to claim the plots cultivated since 1839. They could also claim the house lots they had occupied since the same year. The people claiming the land, however, had to contribute to the costs of surveying the land. Those people who hadn't cultivated any land were given the chance to buy a maximum of fifty acres of government land at a minimum price of fifty cents an acre.

Despite the best efforts to make the distribution fair, only about 35 percent of eligible males received any land. Some people followed through with the procedure to receive land, but many just didn't understand the concept or didn't see why registering a claim was necessary. They didn't understand why anyone should own a resource like land that had been always shared.

The Hawaiian legislature also approved laws that let foreigners buy and sell land. The government thought this would be the best way to introduce a modern economy to the islands. It ignored the fact that the people preferred their old way of life. Even worse, the new land distribution had the effect of transferring land ownership from the Hawaiians to the foreigners.

In the seventy years since Cook's arrival in the Hawaiian Islands, everything had changed. The wisdom of Hawaiian culture was so different from Western society's that the Americans and British could make no sense of it. For their part, the Hawaiians could not withstand the on slaught of Western values, and they let much of their culture's strengths slip through their fingers.

Nevertheless, King Kamehameha III successfully transformed his land into a constitutional monarchy, recognized by other nations around the world. During the years that followed, Hawaii tried to take its place in a world ruled by the Western notions of Christianity and economy. It might have been successful if it weren't for its fertile soil that proved to be so well suited for sugarcane and pineapple. Americans craved the sweet treats Hawaii could provide, and American businesspeople saw the money to be made.

Americans' economic interests in Hawaii, however, would have an earthshaking effect on the islands' politics. Before long, the full force of the Monroe Doctrine would be felt there— and nothing would ever be the same for the islanders.

Of the 4,118,000 acres that were distributed during the "Great Mahele" (land division) of 1848, the native commoners received about 28,658 acres, only about .7 percent. The King and royalty received more, but they were soon selling their land to Europeans and Americans. By the time the monarchy was over-

Three
AN AMERICAN HAWAII

Most of us have eaten Dole pineapple. Few Americans, however, are aware of the major role the Dole family played in Hawaii's history.

In 1851, James Drummond Dole founded the Hawaiian Pineapple Company. As the years passed, Mr. Dole's business grew. Hawaiian Pineapple Company planted, harvested, canned, and shipped pineapple, and eventually, Dole developed the pineapple business into Hawaii's second-largest industry. In achieving his goal of making pineapple available in every grocery store in the country, James Dole made the name "Hawaii" almost **synonymous** with "pineapple."

*To be **synonymous** is to have the same, or nearly the same, meaning as another word.*

Many of the people like Mr. Dole were honest businessmen simply trying to get ahead in the old-fashioned American way. They did not fully comprehend the effect their efforts would have on the native people of Hawaii.

Meanwhile, Great Britain had its own interests in Hawaii. The British landowners living in Hawaii fueled England's hope that Hawaii might pull away from the United States and become part of the British chain that extended from Canada down across the Pacific to Australia. Once again, however, the aging superpower was destined to be challenged by its upstart American offspring. The United States was all

Hawaiian pineapple pickers

grown up now—and it had learned to be assertive about protecting its interests.

Despite the economic and social changes brought by Westerners, the monarchy in Hawaii managed to maintain its power for several generations. The royal family ran into various conflicts with the Westerners over cultural differences (such as marriages between brother and sister, which the Hawaiians perceived as perfectly acceptable), but Hawaiian nobles and their children traveled abroad and received Western-style education. The influence of the United States was especially strong on

Annexation *is the incorporation of a state or territory into another state or territory.*

A **protectorate** *is a country or region defended or controlled by a stronger country.*

Dole's innovative advertising campaign distributed pineapple recipes to ladies' magazines, increasing the fruit's popularity to the point that it was sought by households throughout the United States.

Hawaii's flag

Hawaiian pineapple canners

Kamehameha III, who proposed letting the United States take Hawaii through peaceful ***annexation***. But when the King died in 1854, his successor, Kamehameha IV, favored the British and ordered "all talks of a ***protectorate*** [of the United States] to cease forever."

But stopping the changes in Hawaii wasn't so simple. For many years, the United States had been interested in the islands for their strategic value. As early as 1842, American statesman Daniel Webster announced that while the

Kamehameha IV

Hawaii's bamboo forests

United States would not take Hawaii as a colony, it would resist any colonization attempt on the is-land by the French or the British. Years later, during President Franklin Pierce's administration, the American government negotiated an annexation treaty with Hawaii, but the treaty became *moot* when the Hawaiian ruler who was negotiating with the United States died.

In 1875, King Kalakaua went to Washington, D.C., becoming the first foreign head of state to address a joint session of Congress. Despite his presence, the treaty he helped to negotiate proved to be extremely profitable to American planters and business interests on the islands. Under the treaty, virtually all Hawaiian products would enter the United States *duty-free*. In re-turn, Hawaii pledged not to enter into the same type of agreement with any other country. When the treaty was renewed in 1884, the United States insisted on the exclusive right to use Pearl Harbor as part of the agreement.

Little by little, the economies of Hawaii and the United States were becoming interwoven. When the Hawaiian business community faced opposition within the United States from the American sugar industry, annexation to the United States seemed the best way to secure success for its ventures. The wealthy white planters (relative newcomers to Hawaii) began to look to America as their safety net.

Queen Liliuokalani

This attitude was reinforced when Queen Liliuokalani succeeded her brother on the throne in 1891. Already suspicious of the influence of the planters, Liliuokalani introduced a new constitution that would deprive the minority white population of the special privileges they had been granted by King Kalakaua. At this point, the Americans on the islands represented less than 20 percent of the population, but they controlled more than 80 percent of the Hawaiian Islands' wealth.

In January 1893, the planters and their commercial allies organized a revolt against the Queen. The **coup** was not directed from

*Something that is **moot** is irrelevant or unimportant.*

*An object that is **duty-free** means that taxes do not have to be paid for it to enter the country.*

*A **coup** is the sudden, often violent, overthrow of a government.*

43

*A government that is **provisional** is temporary or conditional pending confirmation.*

*A **republic** is a government in which people elect representatives to exercise power on their behalf.*

*The written statement of a government's organizational structure is called a **constitution**.*

John L. Stevens

Washington, but the U.S. minister to Hawaii, John L. Stevens, collaborated with Hawaiian-born American Sanford B. Dole in staging the rebellion. Stevens ordered American Marines from the U.S.S. *Boston* to land and occupy key government buildings, supposedly to protect the lives and property of U.S. citizens. He also recognized, on behalf of the U.S. government, the ***provisional*** government established by the coup leaders.

The provisional government's representatives arrived in Washington on February 3 and were welcomed by the administration of President Benjamin Harrison. The American government promptly wrote a treaty to annex the islands. But when President Grover Cleveland took office on March 4, the treaty was still in the Senate Foreign Relations Committee.

President Cleveland recognized that the treaty had popular support within the United States, but he also suspected that Stevens had assisted the rebellion. The same man who endorsed the Monroe Doctrine so fervently in South America had a quite different emotional reaction to Hawaii. Uncomfortable with the thought that America had self-servingly influenced political events in the island nation, Cleveland recalled the treaty from consideration by the Senate on March 9.

When the President sent an investigator to the islands to determine what had happened there, he was outraged to learn about the depths of Stevens' involvement in the coup. He replaced Stevens as minister, but Cleveland had limited options. The head of the provisional government, Sanford Dole (who was also the leader of the Safety Committee, which had instigated the coup), insisted that the only choices Cleveland had were either to annex the

Americans involved with the coup

Meanwhile, Hawaii's provisional government was still intent on becoming part of the United States in order to protect its members' financial interests. These men decided that their best hope of achieving this was to form a *republic* in an effort to keep the monarchy from regaining control. Throughout the summer of 1894, they worked to write the new republic's *constitution*.

The finished document resembled the U.S. Constitution in many ways. It provided for executive, legislative, and judicial branches of the government; and it spoke of freedoms of religion, speech, press, and assembly. Unlike the American Constitution, however, these freedoms had certain restrictions attached to them. The constitution of the Republic of Hawaii was designed to protect the American landowners' control of the new government. People were only allowed to vote and hold office if they owned a minimum amount of land, and people could not be considered citizens if they could not read, write, and speak English, as well as explain the constitution in English. This meant that very few Hawaiian natives could vote, and fewer still were eligible to hold a political office.

The constitutional convention concluded by electing Sanford B. Dole, the owner of enor-

islands or recognize his government. For her part, Liliuokalani insisted that she had a right to execute the coup leaders.

Cleveland was stumped. Finally, he submitted the matter to Congress, essentially acknowledging the failure of his diplomacy. After much bitter debate, Congress advised the Cleveland administration to recognize the new minority government, but not to make any further steps to annex the islands.

mous pineapple plantations, as the president of the new nation. Initially, Dole had planned to refuse the presidency and put Princess Kaiulani on the throne instead of her aunt, Queen Liliuokalani. Dole's friends, however, other American landowners like himself, encouraged him to accept the presidency as an opportunity to do "great good" for their own interests, and eventually, he accepted. Within two days, other world nations, including the United States, had recognized the new country.

The republic's new leaders, however, had no interest in remaining an independent nation.

Sanford B. Dole

Today, historians judge Cleveland's policy toward Hawaii to be unsuccessful. Cleveland was concerned about honesty in foreign policy, and yet he failed to follow through on his concerns. In effect, he did not want Hawaii on his conscience—so he left the issues presented by the Hawaiian Islands to be tackled by a future administration.

Instead, they were waiting patiently for Cleveland's term of office to end. The next American president, they hoped, would help them carry through their goal: annexation of Hawaii by the United States.

The new McKinley administration faced other complications, though: war with Spain. Tensions in Cuba, Puerto Rico, and the Philippines diverted America's attention away from its interests in Hawaii.

As things turned out, however, the Spanish-American War provided the nudge America

During much of these events, Queen Liliuokalani had been held under house arrest inside her palace. At the time of the initial coup, she wrote that she yielded "to the superior force of the United States . . . to avoid any collision of armed forces and perhaps loss of life . . . until such time as the Government of the United States shall, upon the facts being presented to it, undo the action of its representatives and reinstate me in the authority which I claim as the constitutional sovereign of the Hawaiian Islands." By the fall of 1895, she was released, and the following year, she received an "absolute pardon" for her "treasonous" activities.

Princess Kaiulani

needed toward Hawaiian annexation. Honolulu was a strategic stopping place for warships headed to the Philippines, and Hawaii did all that it could to make the troops feel welcome. Americans did not want to risk Spain attacking

Hawaii, and new pressure mounted to bring the islands into the American fold.

On August 12, 1898, in front of the building that had once been the royal palace, U.S. Minister Harold Sewell read the annexation resolution. President Dole responded with a short speech in which he yielded to the United States "the sovereignty and public property of the Hawaiian Islands."

Many native Hawaiians refused to attend the annexation ceremony, including Queen Liliuokalani and Princess Kaiulani. Instead, royalists gathered at the Queen's personal residence to console her. For them, it was the saddest day they had ever known.

Sanford Dole transferring Hawaii to the United States

Today the American flag flies over the Hawaiian flag.

Lowering the Hawaiian flag for the last time

In 1993, the U.S. government apologized "to native Hawaiians on behalf of the people of the United States for the overthrow of the Kingdom of Hawaii on January 17, 1893 with the participation of agents and citizens of the United States, and the deprivation of the rights of native Hawaiians to self-determination." For some Hawaiians, this apology is too little too late; activists want nothing less than a return to full Hawaiian sovereignty over the islands. Dr. Kekuni Blaisdell, one of these activists, says, "It's a matter of choosing which status we want: do we remain under the heel of the dominating, exploiting, colonizing United States or do we want to be sovereign?"

Armed troops from the U.S.S. *Mohican* attended the ceremony to make sure that everything went peacefully. The warships in the harbor fired final salutes to the Hawaiian flag, and then it was hauled down while the Hawaiian national anthem played for the last time as the song of an independent nation. Then, while "The Star Spangled Banner" trumpeted across the grounds, the American flag rose over the old palace building.

The U.S. government had plans for shaping Hawaii's new territorial government, but the Spanish-American War would be keeping the country busy for several years. In the meantime, Dole continued to lead Hawaii's government, but now as the governor of the Territory of

> "We have to mend the past so that we can move into the future."
> —John Keola Lake, Hawaiian chanter

Hawaii. With only minor changes, the government of what had been the Republic of Hawaii still managed affairs in the annexed islands. Citizens of the republic were automatically considered citizens of the United States—and those who had been barred from citizenship (including Asians and many native Hawaiians) were now excluded from American citizenship as well.

As England's power began to wane, America stepped into the limelight, flexing her empire-building muscles. Around the world, the Monroe Doctrine was being played out on other islands: Cuba, the Philippines, Guam, and Puerto Rico. Like Hawaii, these islands also had stories of their own.

51

300   Septentrio.

295

C U

B A   INS

S. Georgii

P. Manatis

P. S. Jago

P. S. Maria

Matanca

Za vana

S. Princis

M. Christi

P. S. Andreas

G. des Blasio   Havana

S. Christo

S. Iacol

S. Christophori

Salinas

Al. sbajarno

B. Hondo
xaquo

S. Christophori

Camarco

S. Trinitatis

Tarquino

Jardines de Reyno

Camarco

C. de Crus

P. del Re

P. de S. Anthonio

C. Ligrofo

P. de S. Julian

S. Jago

Jardines S.
Christophori

Melilla

C. de S.
Anthonio

Caiman grande

I. de Lagartes

Sevgilia

Punta
del Negrillo

Oristan   Aguai
pro.

Caimanes

Lago

Occidens.

Mira

El Negrillo

$\mathcal{S}$INUS BUCA

Iamaica I.

Sta nilla

TANUS.   Biboras

Serranilla

C. de Camaron

Serranna

Map of Cuba from 1616

Indies.

Four
CUBA

More than five hundred years ago, a fleet of canoes fled their home for a nearby island.

The travelers' leader, Hatuey, strode up the sandy beach to greet the island's inhabitants.

The tale he told them made the people tremble.

Hatuey told of light-skinned men dressed in shiny metal, carrying weapons harder than stone, who thought nothing of beheading a child for sport, who ordered dogs to tear open other men's stomachs, and who chopped off the hands and feet of Hatuey's people and left the bodies in the bloody dirt to die. These men, he said, treated other human beings worse than they treated animals. They would come to this island, Hatuey warned, preaching about a forgiving (and white-skinned) god. They would say that all they did was for the glory of this god. But really, Hatuey proclaimed, their god was gold, and all their horrific deeds were part of a crazy lust for the yellow metal. Hatuey urged the island's people to join him and flee into the mountains. From there, he said, they could attack these horrible men when they came and

Atrocities are extremely cruel acts, often committed during times of war.

Baptized means to be admitted into Christianity through a religious rite, usually involving sprinkling with or immersion into water.

A **martyr** is a person who is put to death for refusing to renounce a faith, belief, or principle.

Landing of the Spanish

Columbus's arrival in the Western Hemisphere

drive them from the island before it was destroyed as Hatuey's own home had been.

The island's inhabitants listened to Hatuey's tale, but few could believe it was true. Yes, they knew of these light-skinned men; a few had already visited the island and even seized some of its people. But how could any human behave as Hatuey described? Hatuey's people marched into the mountains, but few of the island's inhabitants followed.

Hatuey, however, was right. The men did come with their armor, swords, dogs, and god. The **atrocities** began, and from their hideaways in the mountains, Hatuey's people fought. It was the is-

Cuba is the largest island in an archipelago, or group of islands, that makes up the modern-day Republic of Cuba. Cuba is located about ninety miles (approximately 150 kilometers) south of Florida and has an area of approximately 43,000 square miles (111,000 square kilometers), making it slightly smaller than the state of Pennsylvania.

land's first revolution, but it failed. Hatuey was captured and sentenced to be burned at the stake. Just before his death, Hatuey's executioners offered him a chance for redemption. If he were to accept their god and agree to be **baptized**, the executioners explained, he would go to heaven to live with their god in everlasting peace. Hatuey thought about the proposition and then asked one question: did these light-skinned men go to heaven as well? The executioners assured him that yes, any good Christian goes to heaven. Hatuey made his decision. If these cruel men were to be found in heaven, then he wished to have no part of it. The fire was lit, and Hatuey became a **martyr** for his people.

Hatuey's legendary struggle and death occurred on an island called Cuba. This island, like the rest of the land in the Western Hemisphere, was changed forever in 1492, when Christopher Columbus, an Italian-born explorer working for the Spanish crown, landed on shores previously unknown to the inhabitants of the Eastern Hemisphere.

Columbus believed he had traveled full circle around the world and landed in the Indies, a part of Asia. Really, however, he had landed in the Bahamas in the Caribbean Sea. He explored a number of the islands, seized some of the people he encountered, and returned to Spain with lavish tales of a land heavy with gold, perfumed with spices, and teeming with people who would make perfect slaves.

Columbus returned to the Caribbean, and many other Spaniards followed. Here, they

Cuba's Spanish heritage is evident in its architecture.

found peaceful *Arawak* peoples living in the hundreds of thousands (perhaps even in the millions), who offered food, friendship, guidance, and their possessions. Columbus, his men, and those who followed enslaved, tortured, and murdered these native people. In just two years, hundreds of thousands of the native islanders had been killed at the hands of the newcomers, by the foreign diseases the Spanish carried, or by suicide—their only escape from the invaders. Within fifty years, only a few hundred of these people remained. In 150 years, perhaps every Arawak was dead.

In 1511, less than twenty years after Columbus's first arrival, the legendary Hatuey gathered his remaining people and fled the island of Hispañiola (the first island occupied by the Spanish) for neighboring Cuba. What happened on Hispañiola, however, was repeated throughout the Americas as Spain seized these hitherto unknown lands.

In Cuba, as in the rest of the Caribbean, the Spanish hoped to find vast amounts of gold to finance their *colonial* aspirations. They soon learned that Columbus's reports were greatly exaggerated, and the island's gold was quickly depleted. To make money off the newly colonized land, they sold thousands of the Arawak as slaves, but with the Arawak dying so promptly, the slave trade would not hold out for long. Nevertheless, Cuba became extremely important to Spain. Its location within 150 miles (240 kilometers) of both Florida and Mexico made it a key part of Spain's trade routes and the perfect launching pad for colonial expeditions further into the Americas.

Soon the Spanish realized a new way Cuba could make them rich. As the settlers exterminated the native population, they seized the fertile farmland and learned to cultivate the native crops. But the Spanish also discovered that another crop would grow well in Cuba: sugarcane. They imported the cane (sugarcane came originally from Asia), and huge plantations were built. Sugar

*The **Arawak** were the native people of the Caribbean and northern and western South America. The Arawak tribes of Cuba were the Ciboney and the Tainos.*

__Colonial__ has to do with a period of time characterized by the seizing of colonies and exploitation of their people by other countries.

Harvesting sugarcane

Cuba's lush land

Stratified *means divided into different levels arranged according to a hierarchy.*

A hybrid *is something made up of a mixture of different elements.*

was Cuba's new gold, and thousands of workers were needed to tend the massive crops. Just as they had once enslaved the Arawak people and kidnapped them to sell in Europe, the Spanish now enslaved people from Africa to work Cuba's plantations.

Within three hundred years of Columbus's arrival, a new Cuban population had replaced the original Arawak peoples. Four main groups made up this deeply **stratified** society: Spanish, *criollo*, African, and *mulatto*. The Spanish held the most powerful positions in Cuba, namely state, church, and military positions. Many

58

came to the Americas hoping to make a name for themselves in the colonies and then move up to more important positions back in Europe. The criollos were Cuban-born people of Spanish descent. Whereas the Spanish controlled the political and military power, the criollos, who were mostly farmers and merchants, controlled much of Cuba's wealth. There were also African slaves, and some of the Africans, Spanish, and criollos mixed. Cuban people of mixed heritage were called mulattos, a rather unkind term as it comes from the Spanish word for mule (a *hybrid* animal). Cuban people of African, criollo, and mulatto descent resented the Spaniards' authority and continued control over the island.

Hatuey had launched the first Cuban revolution in the 1500s and failed. By the mid-1800s,

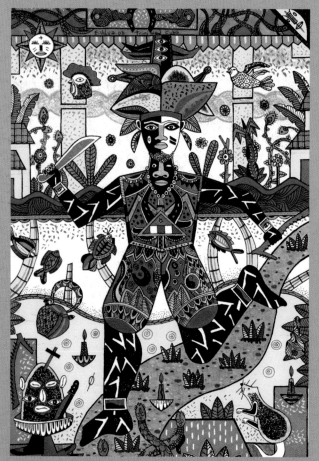

African roots influence modern Cuban artwork and religion.

Cuba's population still wanted freedom from its colonial overlord. Cubans, however, were divided over what independence from Spain should mean. Some Cubans, especially free blacks, slaves, and mulattos, thought Cuba should become completely independent. Many criollos, whose farms depended on slave labor and who feared an uprising of Cuba's black population, wanted to remain part of Spain for the protection its military forces could provide. Others, again mostly well-to-do criollos, wanted Cuba to be annexed to the United States, who was now Cuba's largest trading partner.

By the early 1890s, more than two decades of civil war and rebellion had devastated Cuba. More than 208,000 Spanish and 50,000 Cubans were killed in a rebellion that ended in 1878, but in 1895, another rebellion began in the rural and mountainous eastern part of the island. This time, the Spanish hit back—hard. In 1897, a personal representative of President William McKinley visited the island and described it like this:

> I traveled by rail from Havana to Matanzas. The country outside of the military posts was practically depopulated. Every house had been burned, banana trees cut down, cane fields swept with fire and everything in the shape of food destroyed.

Some of this was the result of the policies of General Valeriano Weyler, who introduced a

60

policy of forcibly moving peasants from the countryside to **deten-tion camps**. The general's goal was to deprive rebels of support from the countryside, but the policy cost thousands their lives and earned Weyler the nickname "Butcher." General Weyler's policies displaced an estimated 400,000 people. Americans saw these events as yet another example of Spain's brutality toward its most important remaining colony in the Western Hemisphere.

Spain had once owned most of South America and much of North America, but over the years, one by one it had lost control of most of its colonies. For the Spanish military, holding on to Cuba had now become an overpowering obsession. Meanwhile, the Spanish government at home faltered and the economy weakened.

The United States did not have a direct interest in the struggle between Spain and the residents of Cuba, but considerable sympathy for the rebel cause existed in the United States. Americans lacked much understanding of the Cuban culture, however.

As far back as 1868, rebels in Cuba had sought to be annexed by the United States. That plan foundered, however, because the rebels refused to **renounce** slavery. Another rebellion in 1878 was planned by a group of Cubans who had moved to the United States.

In the last decades of the nineteenth century, the United States was closely linked economically to Cuba. By 1894, American imports from Cuba were three times the imports from all other Latin American countries, and as a source of all imports to the United States, Cuba was exceeded by only Great Britain. Cuban exports to the United States were 87 percent of the country's total exports. The United States was the destination for most of the island's sugar exports.

Detention camps are prison camps.

*To **renounce** something is to reject or disavow it.*

President McKinley

Cuba also had military value to the United States because of its location. The northwest coast of Cuba lies only ninety miles from Key West, Florida. Cuba also held an important strategic position in the Caribbean.

President Grover Cleveland had proclaimed **neutrality** in the conflict between Cuba and Spain, and he forbid American citizens to engage in activities directed against the established government of Cuba. The policy, however, benefited Spain, even as Cleveland energetically defended the rights of American citizens in Cuba. By the time he left office, Cleveland was almost certain that a war with Spain over the issue of Cuba would be impossible to avoid. The case for war was strengthened by the American public's emotional response to the reports of atrocities committed by the Spanish Army.

When President William McKinley took office after Cleveland, he had no desire to get involved in a fight with Spain. McKinley had served as a captain in the American Civil War, and he knew how terrible war could be. However, he was strongly pressured by events, a pro-war **faction** of the Republican Party, and the **sensationalist** newspapers of the time.

At the end of the nineteenth century, the publishing world was using new technology that allowed more effective use of illustrations with news stories. This provided readers with more **lurid** news coverage. As war tensions increased, William Randolph Hearst, publisher of the *Journal*, was locked in a New York City circulation war with Joseph Pulitzer, publisher of the *World*.

When the crisis in Cuba developed, the newspapers of the day covered it dramatically. The *World*, for example, published large pictures of starving Cuban children on its front page, illustrating the horrors of General Weyler's policies. When the daughter of a Cuban rebel leader was to be **deported** to a Spanish prison colony, the *Journal* launched a campaign to "enlist the women of America" to save her. Famous women such as Julia Ward Howe (the founder of the American Girl Scouts) and President McKinley's own mother signed on to the effort.

The newspapers were **biased** against the Spanish; although the rebels also committed their share of brutalities, those were barely mentioned. And the newspaper coverage did not wait patiently for all the facts to be discovered before making conclusions about who was at fault.

Probably the most obvious example of this bias was the rush to blame Spain for the explosion of the U.S.S. *Maine* on February 15, 1898. After the explosion, the *Journal* promptly proclaimed, "The War Ship Maine Was Split in Two by an Enemy's Secret Infernal Machine!" The explosion of the *Maine* was not the real reason for the Spanish-American War, but it provided the final nudge the American government needed to plunge into war.

McKinley and others were reluctant to declare war, and they made some attempts at negotiation with Spain. A key demand of

Neutrality is the state of not taking sides in a conflict.

*A **faction** is a subgroup whose interests do not always agree with the larger group.*

*Something that is **sensationalist** has placed excessive emphasis on the most shocking aspect of a subject.*

*If something is **lurid**, it is shocking and told in graphic detail.*

*Someone who is **deported** is banished from the country in which he lived.*

*To be **biased** is to be unfair or partial because of a preference for or dislike of something or someone.*

Cuba's lush land

Socialites are people who are well known in society.

When Hearst bought New York City's *Journal* in 1895, it had a circulation of 30,000; by 1897, it was selling more than 400,000 copies daily. During the Spanish-American War, its circulation could exceed one million.

William Randolph Hearst

the Americans was that Spain recognize the independence of Cuba. But Spain refused to do this, and on April 11, 1898, McKinley's war message was read in the House of Representatives. On April 20, he approved Congress's resolution ordering Spain to leave Cuba.

President McKinley may have been slow to go to war, but his assistant secretary to the navy, Theodore Roosevelt, had a different perspective. Ever since he was a child, Roosevelt had loved the thrill of combat. As a boy, he read military histories avidly, and as a young man, he wrote a respected naval history.

As soon as war with Spain was declared, Roosevelt resigned his position as assistant secretary of the navy to serve as lieutenant colonel in the First U.S. Volunteer Calvary—the "Rough Riders," as the troops were soon known. The regiment consisted of both cowboys and *socialites*, and Roosevelt was put in charge of training the men to fight together, a daunting task. The members of the new regiment were used to riding polo ponies, but now they rode half-wild mounts. When the regiment arrived in Cuba, however, it discovered that the campaign was to be on foot. Only two horses were kept, which Roosevelt took turns riding as he directed the troops' advances.

While the U.S. Army was slogging in the mud toward Santiago, the U.S. Navy was assembling in Cuban waters. By early summer, the American forces began their battles with the Spanish defenders. Both sides fought fiercely. Though the Americans had more men, the Spanish had their own advantages; for example, they used smokeless gunpowder, which allowed them to fire on the Americans without showing their locations.

But the Spanish troops were poorly commanded, and they made a number of bad strategic moves. The Americans took Las Guasimas

Wreck of the U.S.S. Maine

65

Theodore Roosevelt

While some military officials criticized Roosevelt for grandstanding, others noted that he showed real leadership in the battles fought by the regiment. He led the Rough Riders in the battle for San Juan Hill, which overlooked the main road into Santiago. Capture of this hill allowed the infantry and artillery forces to set up the final siege of that city, which led to the war's final victory.

But Roosevelt had his own criticisms of the top brass in the U.S. Army. When the fighting ended, Roosevelt said the high command did not evacuate the troops fast enough, when many were dying of malaria. He organized a "round-robin" letter to the Associated Press, demanding that the soldiers be taken from Cuba. There was talk of a court-martial for Roosevelt, but no one wanted to challenge him so soon after he had earned war hero status.

The Battle of San Juan Hill

Yellow fever *is a viral disease transmitted by mosquitoes and is characterized by high fever, hemorrhaging, vomiting of blood, and liver damage.*

Reciprocal trade *refers to exchange between countries.*

on June 23 and then San Juan Hill on July 1. The battles, however, exhausted the American soldiers, who didn't then have the strength to take Santiago, less than a mile away. Finally, however, after several more weeks of battle, Santiago surrendered.

General Leonard Wood, who had commanded the Rough Riders and the 2nd Cavalry Brigade, was ordered to help the starved and suffering city of Santiago. About two hundred people were dying every day, and there was neither space nor means to bury them all. Instead, pyres of corpses were erected and burned, creating black clouds of smoke over the city.

Conditions in the city did improve, but the health of the American troops still stationed in the area got worse. By the end of July, at least 3,370 Americans were ill; by August 2, the names of 4,290 soldiers were on the sick list. Many of the sick suffered from the ***yellow fever*** spread by mosquitoes in the area. Health authorities at the time didn't understand the cause of the disease, and

Teddy Roosevelt and the other Rough Riders getting ready to depart for Cuba

they didn't know how to treat it. Clearly, the men needed to come home soon. At last, after many delays, the American troops started leaving Santiago for home.

When the Spanish-American War finally came to an end, the United States occupied Cuba under the terms of the peace treaty signed in Paris. On February 17, 1901, the U.S. Senate passed the Platt Amendment, which gave the United States an open-ended right to intervene in Cuban affairs. The Cuban government was prohibited under the law from allowing any other country other than the United States to use the island for military purposes. While the Cubans, understandably, objected to this condition on their independence, the United States firmly refused to consider granting the island independence unless the Platt Amendment became part of the new nation's constitution. The Cuban constitutional convention refused to incorporate the amendment at first, but after long negotiations and promises of a ***reciprocal trade*** treaty, the delegates voted sixteen to eleven to accept it. For the time being, Cuba was firmly under America's thumb.

Meanwhile, the effects of the Spanish-American War were being felt in another island nation far away in the Pacific.

American ships departing for Manila

Five
THE PHILIPPINES

On April 25, five days after President McKinley approved Congress's resolution ordering Spain from Cuba, he also approved its declaration of war against Spain, Admiral George Dewey received a cable from the secretary of the navy: "War has commenced between the United States and Spain. Proceed at once to Philippine Islands. Commence operations particularly against the Spanish fleet. You must capture vessels or destroy. Use utmost endeavor."

In the years before the outbreak of war with Spain, few Americans could have told you where the Philippines were. For centuries, the United States had largely ignored this group of islands in the Pacific. But the Filipinos were an ancient people with a culture that had endured for centuries.

Thousands of years ago, the people from various locations in Asia had crossed the Pacific to settle the Philippine Islands. Over the years, these people had intermarried, creating a diverse and culturally rich group of people. As a free and independent people, the early Filipinos carried on trade with Borneo, Celebes, Java, Sumatra, and other countries of Southeast Asia. The islands' proximity to India meant that the culture of this nation cast its influence over the

Colonizers are people who establish colonies in another place.

Rajas are kings, princes, or chiefs among some peoples of Southeast Asia.

If something is owned **communally**, all members of the group or society own it.

The **elite** are the people of a community who have more power, wealth, and social standing.

Philippines as well. Like many societies around the world, however, things changed drastically with the coming of the European **colonizers**.

Ferdinand Magellan had left Spain in 1519 on the first voyage to circle the globe. He set out with five ships and 264 crewmen. Three years later, only one of his ships and eighteen men returned to Spain. The Philippine Islands had proved to be the death of Magellan.

Magellan arrived in the Philippines in 1521. Originally, he was welcomed to the islands by two *rajas*. He named the islands the Archipelago of San Lazaro, erected a cross, and claimed the lands for Spain. Magellan then agreed to help one of the friendly rajas in his fight against rebellious warriors on a nearby island—but Magellan died during the battle between Spanish soldiers and native warriors.

Ferdinand Magellan

The *sarong* (skirt) and *potong* (turban) of the pre-Spanish Filipinos and the embroidered shawls of the present-day Muslim Filipino women reveal Indian influences, and the ancient Filipino alphabet originated from India. About 25 percent of the words in the Tagalog language (the language of the Philippine Islands) are Sanskrit terms originating from India.

ton cargo of cloves sold for a small fortune, and Spain sent out four more expeditions between 1525 and 1542. The commander of the fourth expedition, Lopez de Villalobos, named the islands after Philip, heir to the Spanish throne.

But the Philippines were not formally organized as a Spanish colony until 1565, when Philip II appointed the island's first Spanish governor. In 1595, Manila became the capital of the colony because of its natural harbor and the fertile land that surrounded it.

Spain's rule had two enduring effects on the Philippines: the people of the islands converted to Roman Catholicism and a class of wealthy landowners was established. Philip II commanded that the conversion of the Filipinos to Christianity was not to be accomplished by force, and so missionaries allowed the new believers to incorporate many of their native customs and rituals into their practice of Christianity. Meanwhile, the Spanish stayed in Manila and governed the islands indirectly through the traditional village chiefs. The Filipino people had originally used the land *communally*, but the Spaniards' influence led to a class of landed nobility that wielded considerable local authority. By creating a privileged land-holding *elite* on whom most of the rural

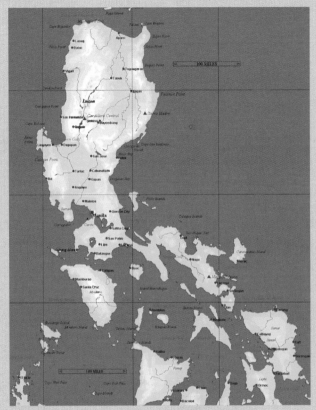

Map of the Philippines

Disagreements over women caused relations to deteriorate still more. More Spaniards died in a skirmish, and the Europeans left the islands and resumed their explorations. Eventually, they limped back home to Spain.

For all its losses, the voyage proved to be a huge financial success. The remaining ship's 26-

population was dependent as landless tenants, Spain introduced a class division in Philippine society that would cause social discontent and political strife for years to come. Spain governed the colony for two hundred years, keeping the islands almost completely isolated from the rest of the world.

When Spain acquired the Philippines, it emerged as a mighty empire—a world power— whose colonies stretched across both hemispheres. Down through history, however, all empires have proved to be impossible to maintain indefinitely. Spain's was no exception. As the years went by, the aging empire found its grasp on the faraway islands weakening.

As the Spanish-American War got under way, an attack on the Philippines was part of America's strategic plan. The idea was to strike where Spain was weak, creating a quick military victory.

Admiral George Dewey took his ships to Manila Bay. His squadron was composed of high-quality ships and arms, and the Spanish forces seriously underestimated it. On an April morning in 1898, his ships sailed right into Manila Bay, attracting only minimal gunfire. So began the first important U.S. naval action

Admiral Dewey at the Battle of Manila

against a foreign foe since the War of 1812. By noon, it was essentially over. Dewey's squadron had destroyed or sank all the Spanish ships. The Spanish had lost 161 men and had 210 wounded. The Americans lost one man from heat stroke; nine were wounded. Americans hailed Dewey as a hero. The Spanish admiral was court-martialed.

Defeating the Spanish fleet in Manila Bay, however, was simpler than seizing the Philippines, or even Manila. In fact, at the highest levels, the American government wasn't entirely clear what its objectives were in the Philippines. President McKinley said the two American objectives were "completing the reduction of Spanish power" and "giving order and security to the islands while in the possession of the United States." Dewey, however, considered the mission to be taking and holding Manila.

As in Cuba, the natives of the Philippines had been fighting their Spanish masters for years. And as in Cuba, the Americans had already been in touch with some of the rebels. A Filipino named Emilio Aguinaldo, one of the *insurgent* leaders, proposed an alliance. In return for arms, the rebels would give two Philippine provinces and *customs collection* to the United States. The U.S. Department of State squelched the deal, but the rebels and Dewey continued to work together. The rebels surrounded Manila on land, and Dewey's ships blockaded the city from the sea.

Aguinaldo, however, made numerous political statements as his forces advanced. He expressed his intention to form an independent government throughout the 7,000-island archipelago. By the end of June, the rebel leader had declared independence for the country and formed a government.

*An **insurgent** is someone who rebels against authority.*

***Customs collection** refers to the collection of taxes on imports.*

Emilio Aguinaldo

75

*A **consul** is a government official who lives in a foreign country and who promotes the commerce of her own state and helps to protect that state's citizens visiting abroad.*

At first the relationship between Aguinaldo's rebels and the Americans was cordial, but the United States was firmly opposed to granting immediate independence to the new government. Meanwhile, the Spanish had decided that they would rather surrender to the Americans than to the rebels.

But the Spanish military governor faced a dilemma. If he just surrendered, he could be court-martialed for cowardice. But the

Guam

Even before the American forces took the Philippines, the war between Spain and the United States led to the acquisition of new lands overseas for the Americans.

Guam, the largest of the Mariana Islands, was important for its location, about two-thirds of the way from Hawaii to the Philippines and within easy sailing distance to Shanghai, Canton, Yokohama, and Hong Kong.

The capture of Guam by the Americans was peaceful, if strange. When the U.S.S. *Charleston* fired a few shots at abandoned forts on the island, two local dignitaries rowed out to the American ship. Unfortunately, they explained, they were unable to respond to what they interpreted as a salute. The captain of the *Charleston* explained that in fact Spain and the United States were at war, and he was attacking the island; furthermore, the two officials were now under arrest. After some formalities, the governor of the island and fifty-six Spanish marines surrendered. Guam became America's newest overseas colony.

On August 13, both Spanish and Americans began to make a show of fighting. Perhaps they were a bit too enthusiastic: the Americans actually suffered more casualties in the fake battle for the city than they did in the real battle for Manila Bay. But the fight achieved its objective. The Spanish surrendered after the battle, and the Americans raised their flag. The Americans then prevented the insurgent Filipinos from entering the city, and while this provoked some bloodshed, Aguinaldo decided not to further challenge the Americans.

When the news of Dewey's victory reached home, Americans cheered, overwhelmed with pride in their nation's achievement. Dewey, "the conqueror of the Philippines," became an instant national hero, and stores soon filled with merchandise bearing his image. Few Americans knew what and where the Philippines were, but the newspapers assured them that the islands were welcome possessions.

Still, America was not quite sure what to do with the Philippines. President McKinley himself said he had a "natural revulsion" to acquiring huge territories like the Philippines so far from the United States—but some of his advisers saw advantages in annexing the Philippines. They could be useful commercially, for example,

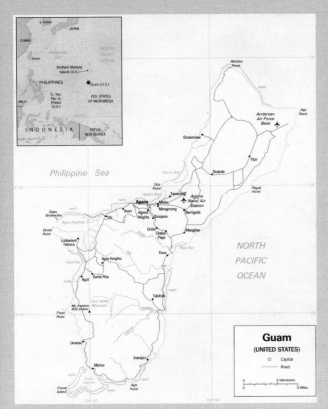

Map of Guam

70,000 surrounded residents of Manila were facing starvation. With the help of the Belgian *consul* in the Philippines, the two sides arrived at a solution. The Americans and the Spanish would pretend to fight, and then the Spanish would surrender. Naturally, the rebels were not consulted.

Aguinaldo (center seated) and the other delegates to the Filipino Assembly of Representatives

and they would certainly come in handy for establishing a naval base in the area. Public opinion also favored some sort of American ownership of the islands. After all, had not the victory of Dewey in Manila Bay decisively ended the rule of Spain in the islands?

Meanwhile, the rebellion of the native Filipinos continued to fester. American diplomats had promised them independence, but now it became obvious that they were empty promises. President McKinley, however, did not consider the Filipinos ready for self-government. If the land was allowed to remain in the natives' hands, he feared the area could descend into chaos—or that another powerful country might take advantage of the situation to seize territory in the Philippines.

Also, while the Philippines were not necessarily valuable economically in themselves, they did have strategic value from a military and trade perspective. The United States was actively looking to expand its commerce into Asia, and the Philippines could serve as a commercial stepping-stone as well as a military and political lever. The business community actively lobbied to retain the Philippines for this purpose. In the words of one business magazine at the time, ownership of the islands would encourage "the teeming millions of the Middle Kingdom [China] to buy largely from us."

At last, faced with difficult choices, McKinley decided "there was nothing left for us to do but to take them all, and to educate the Filipinos, and uplift and civilize and Christianize them."

The Filipinos already had their own form of Christianity, and they were not eager to be uplifted and civilized according to America's terms. However, after three years of resistance, Aguinaldo, the rebel leader, finally gave in and made an oath of allegiance to the U.S. government; he also issued a proclamation, asking his fellow rebels to surrender. "The time has come," said Aguinaldo, "when they [the Filipino people] find their advance along this path impeded by an irresistible force. Enough of blood, enough of tears and desolation."

This Filipino has his own story to tell.

Building an empire did not come cheap for either side. The three-year rebellion had cost the United States the lives of 4,234 soldiers, while about 20,000 Filipino soldiers had been killed in the fight. At home, however, Americans were filled with pride in their growing nation. The Spanish-American War had proved to be a "splendid little war" (as one of Teddy Roosevelt's friends said).

The tally of American gains was still not complete, however. Across the world, yet another island nation had expanded U.S. boundaries.

Six
PUERTO RICO AND THE AMERICAN EMPIRE

The Spanish-American War reached Puerto Rico only seventeen days before Spain surrendered. The American general informed Puerto Ricans:

> We have not come to make war upon the people of a country that for centuries has been oppressed but on the contrary to bring you protection . . . to promote your prosperity, and to bestow upon you the immunities and blessings of the liberal institutions of our government.

Puerto Rico was not entirely reassured by these words. Its people worried they would become an American colony. Seven years earlier, they had finally won from Spain the right to much of their own government—and they were not looking for a new master. After all, they had been under Spain's thumb for more than four hundred years.

In 1493, Christopher Columbus found Puerto Rico by accident, when his men saw twelve frantic young women and two young boys on a small island, near the island that would later be called Puerto Rico. Columbus's ships had traveled from Spain to a chain of islands in the Caribbean Ocean, about a thousand miles southeast of Florida. The young people his crew found there were Arawak, escaped prisoners in flight from another tribe.

The Arawak appeared strange to Columbus and his men. Their skin was the color of copper, and they were much shorter than the Spaniards, with straight black hair and prominent cheekbones. They wore jewelry of shells, bones, clay, and gold, but except for the married women, the Arawak wore no clothes.

Columbus and his men must have looked equally strange to the Arawak. The seventeen wooden ships rose high out of the water, carrying at least 1,200 men, men who wore heavy armor and used weapons such as swords and pistols. The peaceful Arawak had never imagined such weaponry, nor could they comprehend the Spanish desire for gold.

On that long-ago day, the Arawak led Columbus through a series of islands toward a

Christopher Columbus

Acquiring Puerto Rico had not been part of America's original plans during the Spanish-American War, but it made good sense strategically. With the annexation of the island, the United States could control the Atlantic approach to the Panama Canal (still unbuilt but a very real idea in some Americans' minds).

larger one, and as Columbus's ships approached it, the young natives dove off his ships toward the beaches that led to their homes. Columbus had arrived on the island we know today as Puerto Rico.

After 1493, Columbus left, and no one from Spain returned for fifteen years. Then, in 1508, a Spaniard named Ponce de Leon returned to build a fort and to colonize the island for Spain. Not only did the Spanish claim the island, but they claimed the Arawak too. King Ferdinand assigned both land and thirty to three hundred Indians to each of the Spanish colonists. Two

The Arawak finally began to rebel against their Spanish masters in 1510, after the natives held a Spaniard under water for several hours to discover if he could actually be killed. They watched his body for several days for signs of life, and then the Arawak revolted on various parts of the island. Ultimately, Ponce de Leon put down the rebellion and ordered six thousand of the Arawak shot. By 1514, with many of the Arawak either dead from disease, killed, or escaped to other islands, less than four thousand of the original 30,000 inhabitants of the island remained. In 1521, when the Spanish King

The Arawak

years later, the Spanish began to mine gold on the island, forcing the natives to do the actual work, to wear clothes, and to study Christianity.

For several years, the Indians worked for the Spanish because they believed the Spanish were immortal. After all, the Spaniards did not become sick from diseases as frequently as the Indians did. (The Spaniards, because they had brought many of the diseases with them from Europe, had built up a resistance to them.)

An Invisible Killer

In the centuries after Columbus landed in the New World in 1492, more native North Americans died each year from infectious diseases brought by the European settlers than were born. Germs were the Indians' worst enemy.

ordered the freedom of all remaining Indians on the island, only six hundred of them were left. When Puerto Rico's gold ran out, the Spanish changed the island's economy from mining to agriculture, and brought in African slaves to work on sugar plantations. Around 1523, sugarcane became the major crop of Puerto Rico, and the Spanish built huge forts to protect the island. By 1572,

A few months after the United States landed in Puerto Rico, the U.S. Congress passed the Foraker Act, describing America's plan for Puerto Rico:

Puerto Rico will at first be governed by a military regime; then it will be declared an American territory, and later it will achieve the category of sovereign state within the Union. The duration of these periods will depend more or less on the merits of the country.

The Foraker Act remained in effect from 1900 to 1916. However, the plans described by the act never came to pass. Unlike Alaska and Hawaii, Puerto Rico never became a state of the United States. Instead, the Foraker Act made the island much like a colony of the United States, the way the original American colonies had belonged to England. The island was not represented in Congress, and it could not refine any of its raw materials, like sugar, that it provided to the United States.

however, Puerto Rico was poor and existed mainly as a military stronghold, protecting against other countries, like England, who now ruled the oceans. Natives, Africans, and Spanish intermarried. For centuries, this new group of people was locked in poverty as Spanish subjects. Now, the nineteenth-century Puerto Ricans would be subject to America's government.

With the end of the Spanish-American War, the United States had the beginning of an empire. Unlike the old empires, America did not wipe out native populations and establish colonies in its new lands. Americans' goal for these lands was to bolster their country's strength in primarily economic ways.

But the acquisition of new territories, even for limited commercial purposes, was a controversial policy in the United States. On the one side of the issue were the **expansionists**—and on the other side were anti-imperialist leagues.

The anti-imperialists were a loose group of people united mainly by their opposition to U.S. expansionism, rather than their support for any particular policy. Ranging from **progressive** to **conservative**, the anti-imperialists feared that the acquisition of colonies overseas would change the character of the United States from its republican origins. The diversity of the group, however, proved to be an obstacle to its success. It was hard for them to work together.

Some were **socialists**, such as Morrison Swift, who charged that the government was under control of big business and that the goal of U.S. foreign policies was the "expansion of billionaires." But some of the wealthiest Americans also opposed U.S. expansion.

__Expansionists__ are people in favor of expanding a country's economy or territory.

Someone who is __progressive__ is in favor of change and is forward-thinking.

A __conservative__ is someone who resists change and likes things the way they are.

__Socialists__ are those who support the political system known as socialism, which favors government control of the distribution of services and goods.

Andrew Carnegie, for example, donated huge amounts of money to the anti-imperialists. Many financial interests feared war and the instability it might bring. Before the hostilities between Spain and the United States escalated into war, the *American Banker* editorialized that "there is not an intelligent, self-respecting and civilized American citizen anywhere who would not prefer to have the existing crisis culminate in peaceful negotiations." Most representatives of labor also opposed imperialist policies. Samuel Gompers, leader of the of American Federation of Labor, feared that annexing Hawaii, for example, would lead to the legalization of the contract labor system used on Hawaiian plantations. Many farmers were concerned that sugar and tobacco produced in the colonies would undercut domestically produced crops.

The opposition to imperialism also had racial and ethnic aspects. Some opponents to the acquisition of colonies feared that brown-skinned people from America's new territories would inundate the Ango-Saxon "race." Some German Americans in the anti-imperialist leagues also feared that the expansion of the United States would lead to conflicts with their homeland.

But a combination of factors bolstered the case for expansion of the United States, and the political leadership and the majority of the public became convinced that expansion was the country's best policy. The acquisition of the Philippines, for example, was described as a wonderful opportunity for missionaries, despite the fact that Christianity had been brought to that land centuries before by Spain. After Dewey's triumph over the Spanish fleet, religious denominations from the Baptists to the Episcopalians referred to occupation of the Philippines as America's "Christian duty." The doctrine of Manifest Destiny also continued to influence Americans' thinking. Originally, the doctrine had described the country's destiny to control the land "from sea to shining sea," but a broader interpretation held that the United States could serve as an unbound force for bringing democracy to new lands.

A shaping force in America's history has been the tension between two opposing attitudes. On one side is the perspective expressed by Manifest Destiny and the Monroe Doctrine, an aggressive patriotism that provides Americans with a sense of pride and identity, reinforcing their belief that they are doing other lands a favor when they interfere in circumstances outside of U.S. boundaries. On the other side is America's ongoing passion for human rights

Political cartoon portraying the "American Empire"

Social activism is the support of policies and practices that benefit society as a whole.

Socialism is the political theory in which the means of production are controlled by the people, and distribution is based on equality, not the marketplace.

and the value of the individual. Both these perspectives were evident at the end of the nineteenth century in the United States.

On the one hand, the nation saw the growth of *social activism* and *socialism*. On the other hand, there was also a sharp increase in expressions of nationalism; during the 1890s, far more patriotic groups were founded than at any other period in the nation's history. In this environment, the ordinary public was persuaded to favor America's "empire" both by calls to patriotism and by emotional appeals to help the people of other lands.

The American story was sounding loud and clear in the ears of its citizens. Filled with national pride and an eagerness to help others less fortunate, most Americans believed their nation's new island possessions would welcome the opportunities the United States offered them. In any case, the United States was growing in power, and its government was not going to rush to release its hold over its newly conquered lands. As the world entered the twentieth century, America's might would continue to grow.

One of Puerto Rico's Spanish forts

1519 Ferdinand Magellan arrives in the Philippines.

1493 Christopher Columbus discovers Puerto Rico.

1795 Chief Kamehameha I unites the Hawaiian Islands.

1778 James Cook lands on the island of Kuai'i; he is killed by island natives in 1779.

1511 Hatuey flees the island of Hispañiola for Cuba.

1823 President James Monroe issues the Monroe Doctrine.

1851 The Dole Company opens the Hawaiian Pineapple Company in Hawaii.

1802 The first sugar mill is opened on the Hawaiian Islands.

1848 Individual ownership of land is allowed for the first time in Hawaii.

February 15, 1898 The U.S.S. *Maine* explodes in the Cuba harbor.

January 17, 1893 The Kingdom of Hawaii is overthrown in a coup, with the participation of agents of the U.S. government.

December 10, 1898 The Treaty of Paris ends the Spanish-American War, and the United States receives the Philippines, Guam, and Puerto Rico.

1875 King Kalakaua becomes the first foreign head of state to address a joint session of Congress.

August 12, 1898 The United States annexes Hawaii.

April 25, 1898 The U.S. Congress declares war on Spain, and the Spanish-American War begins.

1917 Puerto Rican residents are given U.S. citizenship.

February 17, 1901 The U.S. Senate passes the Platt Amendment, giving the United States the right to intervene in Cuban affairs.

1946 The Philippines are granted their independence from the United States.

FURTHER READING

Allen, Helena G. *The Betrayal of Liliuokalani, Last Queen of Hawaii.* Glendale, Calif.: The Arthur H. Clark Company, 1992.

Balfour, Sebastian. *The End of the Spanish Empire, 1989–1923.* Oxford: Clarendon Press, 1997.

Brown, Charles H. *The Correspondents' War: Journalists in the Spanish-American War.* New York: Charles Scribner's Sons, 1967.

Linnéa, Sharon. *Princess Ka'iulani: Hope of a Nation, Heart of a People.* Grand Rapids, Mich.: Eerdmans, 1999.

Musicant, Ivan. *Empire by Default: The Spanish-American War and the Dawn of the American Century.* New York: Henry Holt and Company, 1998.

FOR MORE INFORMATION

Cuba
www.historyofcuba.com
www.unipr.it/~davide/cuba/home/html

Hawaii
www.hawaii.gov/hidocs/hpwebcul.html
www.lava,net/~poda/history.html

Philippines
Workmall.com/wfb2001/Philippines/
Philippines_history_index
www.philippines.hvu.nl

Puerto Rico
Welcometopuertorico.org
www.eia.doe.gov/emeu/cabs/prico.html

Spanish-American War
www.loc.gov/rr/hispanic/1898
www.wccusd.k12.us/elcerrito/history/
span-amerwar.htm

Teddy Roosevelt and the Rough Riders
www.montauklife.com/teddy98.html

Publisher's note:
The Web sites listed on these pages were active at the time of publication. The publisher is not responsible for Web sites that have changed their addresses or discontinued operation since the date of publication. The publisher will review the Web sites and update the list upon each reprint.

INDEX

BIOGRAPHIES

AUTHOR

Eric Schwartz is a journalist living in Binghamton, New York. He received his bachelor's degree in Russian and journalism from Michigan State University and his master's degree in international relations from Syracuse University.

SERIES CONSULTANT

Dr. Jack N. Rakove is a professor of history and American studies at Stanford University, where he is director of American studies. The winner of the 1997 Pulitzer Prize in history, Dr. Rakove is the author of *The Unfinished Election of 2000, Constitutional Culture and Democratic Rule,* and *James Madison and the Creation of the American Republic.* He is also the president of the Society for the History of the Early American Republic.

PICTURE CREDITS

Benjamin Stewart: pp. 19, 20, 22–23, 24 (front), 24–25, 26–27, 31 (front), 32, 33 (front and back), 34–35, 40, 42–43, 49 (front), 50–51
British National Archives: p. 12
Central Intelligence Agency: p. 77
Charles Johnson Post: pp. 66–67, 68–69
Cuban Art Space: p. 60
Hawaiian State Archives: pp. 27 (front), 28–29, 30–31, 38–39, 41 (right and left), 43 (front), 44, 45, 46, 48, 49 (background)
Hemera Image: pp. 12–13, 14, 18
Library of Congress: pp. 17, 75
National Archives and Records Administration: pp. 64–65
Naval Historical Center: p. 70
Photos.com: pp. 8, 9, 10, 36, 79
Roxanna Stevens: pp. 80–81, 84–85, 87 (right)
Viola Ruelke Gommer: pp. 56, 58–59, 62–63
William James Hubbard: p. 16

To the best knowledge of the publisher, all other images are in the public domain. If any image has been inadvertently uncredited, please notify Harding House Publishing Service, Vestal, New York 13850, so that rectification can be made for future printings.

MER du SUD
PACIFIQUE
MER du NORD
Tropique du Capricorne
Terres Antarctiques Australes
Cercle Polaire Antarctique